A Little Kinder Than Necessary

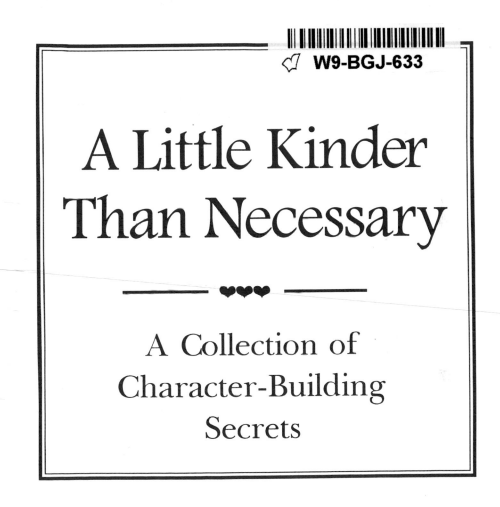

A Collection of Character-Building Secrets

To Carol ~

Kindness is Contagious!

Bud Strong Salvic

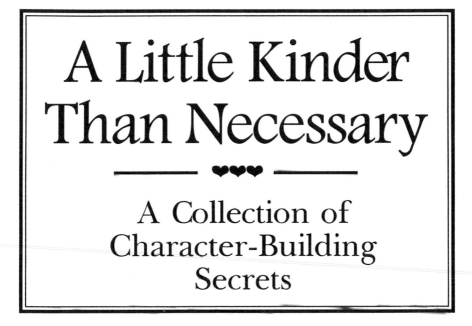

A Little Kinder Than Necessary

A Collection of Character-Building Secrets

Compiled by Beth Strong Taber

Illustrated by Joyce Orchard Garamella

NICOLIN FIELDS
PUBLISHING
INCORPORATED
2456 Lafayette Road, Portsmouth, NH 03801 (603) 422-8772

Printed and bound in Canada. All rights reserved. Published by Nicolin Fields Publishing, Inc., 2456 Lafayette Road, Portsmouth, NH 03801, USA.   nfp@nh.ultranet.com

Cover illustration and interior illustrations by Joyce Orchard Garamella.
Cover design by Mayapriya Long.
Interior design by Linda Chestney.

The quotations contained in *A Little Kinder Than Necessary* were gathered from many different sources over the years. They have been presented as accurately as possible. An intensive search was done to determine if any of the material required permission to reprint. If there have been any errors, please advise and corrections will be made in future editions.

For permission to reprint copyrighted material, we are grateful to the following publishers and authors: (Continued on last page.)

Library of Congress Cataloging-in-Publication Data

Taber, Beth Strong, 1960–
     A little kinder than necessary : a collection of character
  -building secrets / compiled by Beth Strong Taber ; illustrated by
  Joyce Orchard Garamella. -- 1st ed.
          p.   cm.
     Summary: A collection of fifty-two quotations from a variety of sources focusing
  on the importance of character in personal development.
       ISBN 0-9637077-4-4
       1. Conduct of life--Quotations, maxims, etc.--Juvenile literature.
  [1. Conduct of life--Quotations, maxims, etc.]   I. Garamella, Joyce
  Orchard, ill.   II. Title.
  PN6084.C55T33 1998
  170' .44--DC21   98-6503
                                                                          CIP
                                                                           AC

Dedicated to our kids...

For Max, Caroline and Will...
You are each
my Pride,
my Joy,
and my Inspiration.
~BST

For my son, Ben...
a really neat kid!
~JOG

━━━━ ❤❤❤ ━━━━

Acknowledgements

Many wonderful people advised and encouraged me with this project. I found that even a "little" book like this can be a big undertaking... it has been a challenging journey and terrific learning experience!

I am exceedingly grateful to Linda Chestney, my editor, for her patience, vision and friendly nudges that kept the project on track. Additionally, I am very fortunate to have had the opportunity to work with Joyce Garamella, whose talent and creativity brought the pages to life. Thank you both!

I would also like to extend my heartfelt appreciation to the following people who helped in so many ways. Some shared their favorite quotes, some shared their suggestions and expertise: Babe Gambrill, Jackie Jarest, Kathy Street, Pamela Schmitt, Mary R. O'Cullanan, Jeff Kelly, Katherine Williams, Mary Elizabeth McCue, Pam Schwotzer and all the librarians at the North Hampton (NH) Public Library, Mark Lingenfelter, Teresa Fredette, Barbara Tague, Sherry Hoffman, Linda Hillier, Lissy McNamara, Janet Carroll and William Richmond.

Thanks so much to my friends and co-workers for their enthusiastic support, especially Valerie Van Zandt Tarantino and Liz Robinson. Most importantly, my deepest thanks to my dad, my mom, and the rest of my family for their love and constant encouragement.

——————— ❤❤❤ ———————

Preface

Dear Reader,

This book began as a letter to my children in the late 1980s, when they were just babies. My desire was to record some of my own values and observations to share with them as they grew—ideas that would inspire positive behavior and attitudes toward themselves and others and would help them become responsible, caring people.

In addition to my own personal thoughts, I also began collecting other words of wisdom in the form of quotes. They came from many different places... teachers, newsletters, articles, friends, etc., and resulted in a variety of ideas and authors.

It is my hope that you are able to find inspiration and meaning in these words and that you enjoy reading them as much as I enjoyed collecting them!

Fondly,

Beth Strong Taber

Introduction

Before you begin *A Little Kinder Than Necessary*, I would like to draw your attention to the following:

You'll find 52 quotes in this collection with enlightening suggestions added for emphasis and consideration. They can be used in a thought-for-the-week style or any other way you choose. As you read each one, reflect upon what it means to you, how it relates to your life, your attitude and your relationships.

You'll find blank pages in the back of the book to record your own favorite "words of wisdom." Fill 'em up! Be inspired!

You may notice that some of the quotations use the male pronoun only, as in: "Behold the turtle, <u>he</u> makes progress only when <u>he</u> sticks <u>his</u> neck out." Many of these quotes were said or written a while ago when it was more appropriate to use "he," "him," "his," etc., in referring to males *and* females. In order to keep the integrity of the quotes, I have chosen to leave them in their original form. Please note, however, that these quotes have meaning for girls and boys alike! They are meant for *all*.

The ideas contained in these quotes and insights, such as patience, tolerance and integrity, are ones that I continuously strive to practice in my own life, as well as to teach to my children. We are all "works in progress" and should always be trying to be the best we can be!

——— ❤❤❤ ———

A Little Kinder

Than Necessary

Character–istics

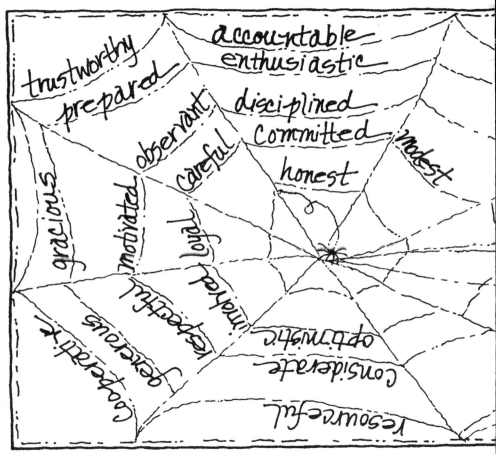

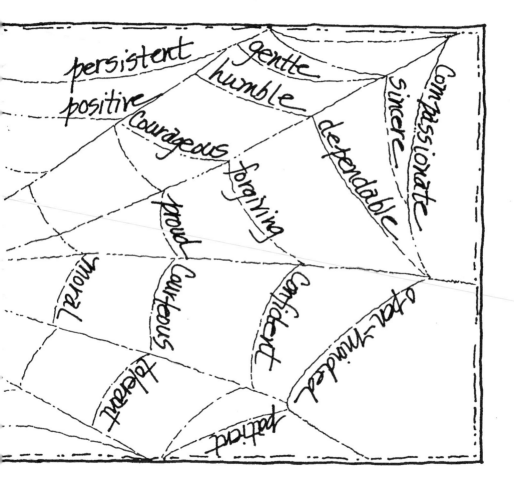

Kind words can be short and easy to speak, but their echoes are truly endless.

Mother Teresa
1910 - 1997
Yugoslavian-born nun
and missionary

The way I see it,
if you want the rainbow,
you gotta put up
with the rain.

Dolly Parton
1946 -
American singer, actress

Hatred paralyzes life;
love releases it.
Hatred confuses life;
love harmonizes it.
Hatred darkens life;
love illuminates it.

Martin Luther King, Jr.
1929 - 1968
American clergyman,
civil rights leader

Better bend
than break.

Scottish Proverb

19

Gratitude is the most
exquisite form
of courtesy.

Jacques Maritain
1882 - 1973
French philosopher, author

Always be
a little kinder
than necessary.

James M. Barrie
1860 ‑ 1937
Scottish actor, author

22

Behold the turtle—
he makes progress
only when he
sticks his neck out.

James B. Conant
1893 - 1978
American educator

When the One Great
Scorer comes to write
against your name,
He marks not that
you won or lost,
but how you played
the game.

Grantland Rice
1880 - 1954
American journalist

The ultimate lesson all
of us have to learn is
unconditional love,
which includes,
not only others,
but ourselves as well.

Elisabeth Kubler-Ross
1926 -
Swiss-born psychiatrist and author

Failure is success
if we learn from it.

Malcolm S. Forbes
1919 - 1990
American billionaire,
publisher, sportsman

Nothing in life
is to be feared;
it is only
to be understood.

Marie Curie
1867 - 1934
Polish-born French chemist
(original name: Manya Sklodowska)

Cornerstones

♥ Do your BEST—but don't concern yourself with being perfect. There is a difference. ♥ Think for yourself. Form your own opinions. ♥ Do the right thing and remember—the right thing is not always popular. The popular thing is not always right. ♥ Attitude is everything —have a great one. ♥ Take responsibility for your actions—be accountable. ♥

♥ Admit your mistakes. Learn from them.
♥ Do not compare yourself to others
and do not worry about what others
think. ♥ Do more than is expected of you
—promise only what you are sure you can
do, then do more than you promise. ♥
Choose your friends and activities
carefully. ♥ Stay away from people who
engage in questionable activities. ♥ If
you want a friend, then BE a friend. ♥

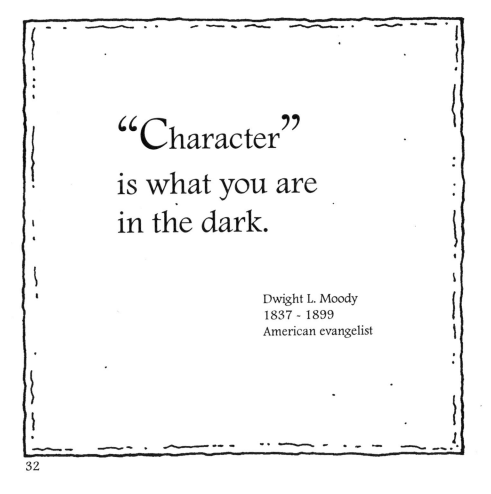

"Character"
is what you are
in the dark.

Dwight L. Moody
1837 - 1899
American evangelist

Practice is the best of all instructors.

Publilius Syrus
1st Century B.C.
Latin author

33

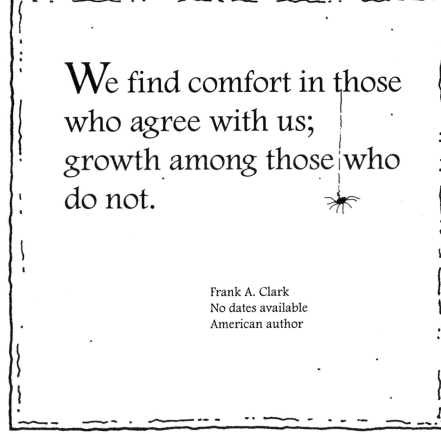

We find comfort in those who agree with us; growth among those who do not.

Frank A. Clark
No dates available
American author

One of the sanest, surest,
and most generous joys
of life comes from being
happy over the good fortune
of others.

Archibald Rutledge
1883 - 1973
American author

Have confidence
that if you have done
a little thing well,
you can do a bigger thing
well, too.

Storey (First name not known)
1819 - 1884
Newspaper editor

36

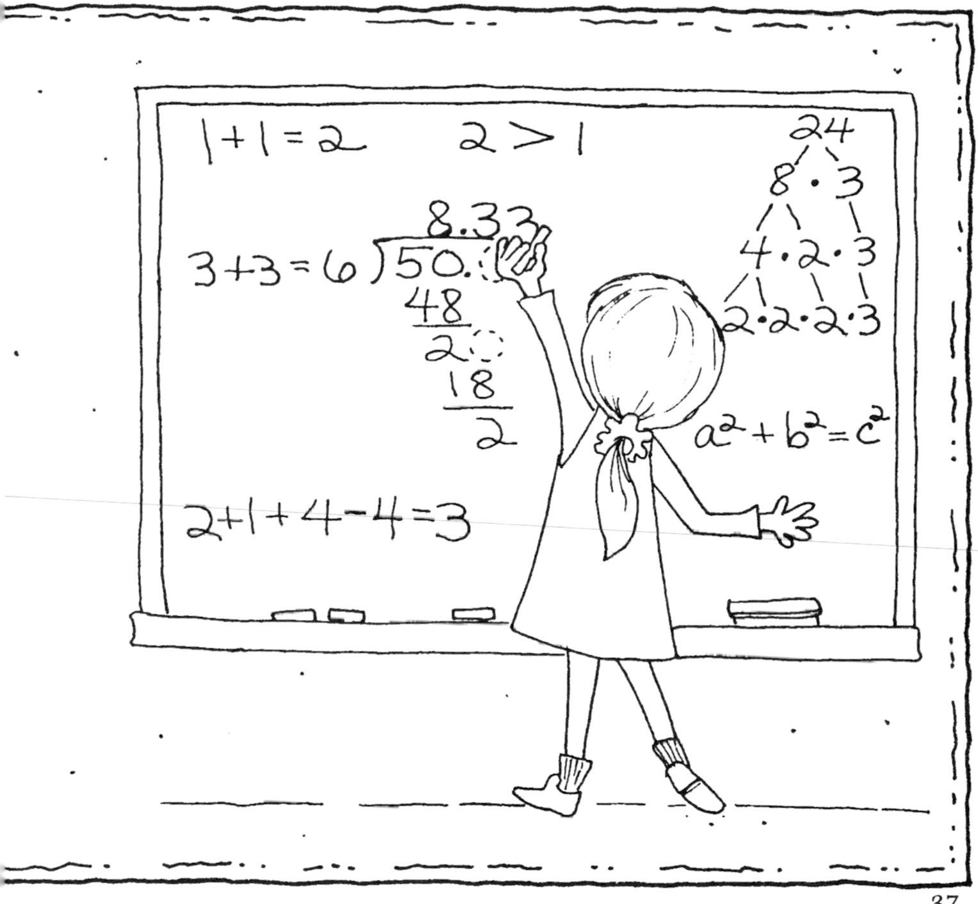

1+1=2
2 > 1
24
8 · 3
4 · 2 · 3
2 · 2 · 2 · 3
8.33
3+3=6) 50.
48
2
18
2
a² + b² = c²
2+1+4−4=3

I think the one lesson I have learned is that there is no substitute for paying attention.

Diane Sawyer
1945 -
American journalist

Skunks Crossing

DETOUR

To be trusted is a greater compliment than to be loved.

George MacDonald
1824 - 1905
Scottish novelist, poet, clergyman,
and children's author

Thinking well is wise.
Planning well is wiser.
Doing well is wisest
and best of all.

Persian Proverb

Never does the human soul appear so strong and noble as when it for~goes revenge and dares to forgive an injury.

Edwin Hubbell Chapin
1814 - 1880
Clergyman, author

Honesty
is the best policy.

Benjamin Franklin
1706 - 1790
American statesperson, author,
inventor, printer, scientist

Do a deed of simple kindness;
though its end you may not see.
It may reach,
like widening ripples,
down a long eternity.

Joseph Norris
1847 - 1916
American author

Works of Heart

♥ Accept others' differences —fight bigotry and prejudice. ♥ Anticipate others' needs—don't wait to be asked.. ♥ Respect other people's opinions. ♥ Teachers, police officers, firefighters, etc. are our heroes—show them respect and gratitude. ♥ Laugh with others, not at others. ♥ Be as courteous to the custodian as you are to the principal. ♥ Be helpful—lend a hand. ♥ Be sensitive—consider other people's feelings. ♥

♥ A "good sport" is a good winner and a good loser. ♥ Treat your brothers and sisters with LOVE and RESPECT. SUPPORT each other. ♥. Respect your elders. — be courteous and patient. ♥ Show respect for yourself and others by using your best manners. ♥ Apologize easily, quickly, and sincerely. ♥ Forgive others. ♥ Look for the best in others. ♥ Be a TEAM PLAYER! ♥ Leave everything better than you found it. Take only pictures— leave only footprints. ♥

Love thy neighbor.

Thales of Miletus
640 - 546 B.C.
Ionian philosopher
One of the Seven Sages of
Greece

Time and words cannot be recalled.

Jean Paul Richter
1763 - 1825
German novelist, aesthetician

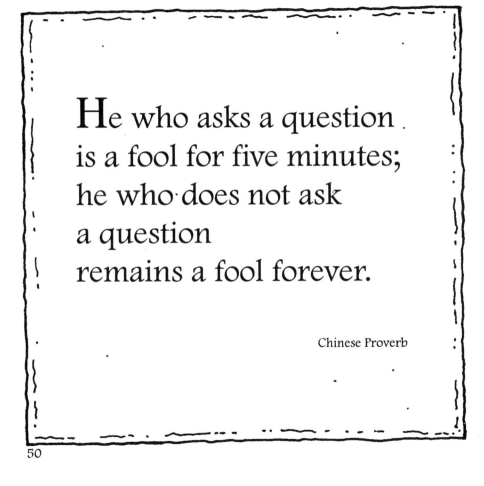

He who asks a question
is a fool for five minutes;
he who does not ask
a question
remains a fool forever.

Chinese Proverb

The pessimist sees the
difficulty in every
opportunity;
the optimist,
the opportunity
in every difficulty.

L.P. Jacks
1860 - 1955
Religious author

You can find a hero
around every corner.

Fred Rogers
1928 -
American television
producer and
host, author

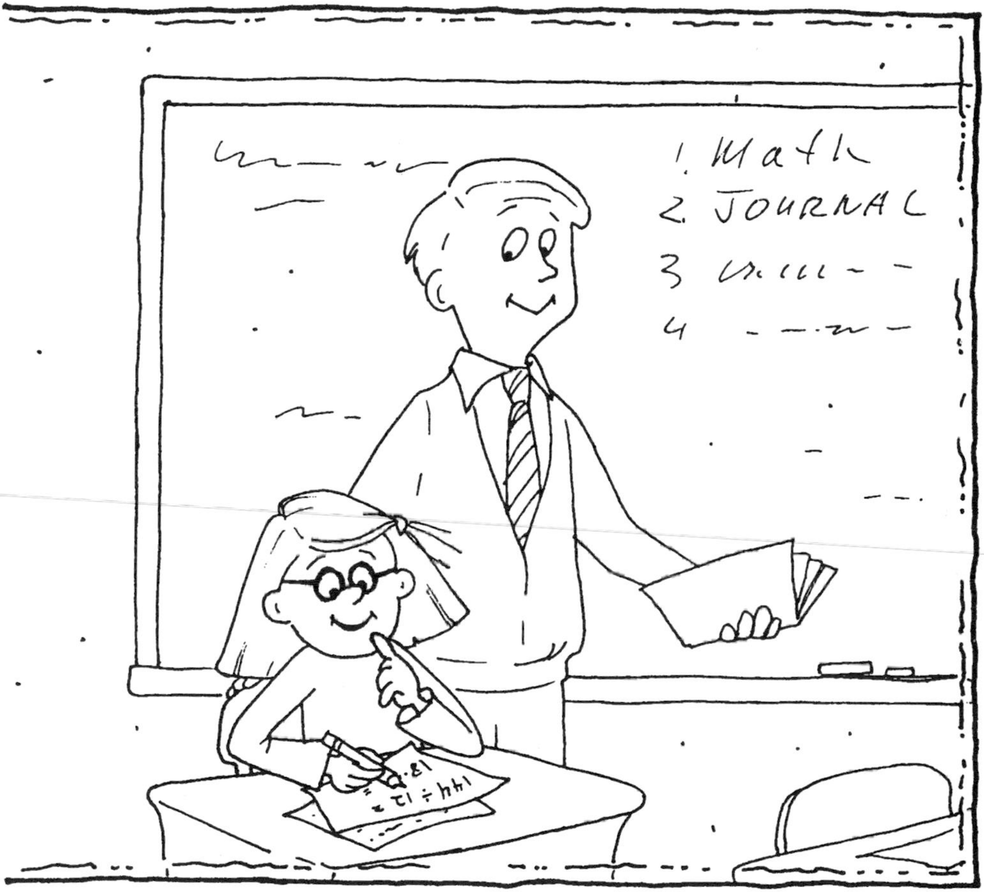
1. Math
2. JOURNAL
3
4
144 ÷ 12 =

...You may be disap-
pointed if you fail,
but you are doomed
if you don't try.

Beverly Sills
1929 -
American opera singer, director

Life is not so short
but that there is
always time enough for
courtesy.

Ralph Waldo Emerson
1803 - 1882
American poet, essayist,
philosopher

Have a heart
that never hardens,
a temper that never tires,
and a touch
that never hurts.

Charles Dickens
1812 - 1870
English author

...The greater part of our happiness or misery depends on our dispositions and not on our circumstances.

Martha Washington
1731 - 1802
American First Lady.

There is little pleasure
in the world that is
sincere and true beside
that of doing our duty
and doing good;
no other is comparable
to this.

John Tillotson
1630 - 1694
Archbishop of Canterbury,
author of sermons and religious writings

Laughter has
no foreign accent.

Paul Lowney
1922 -
American humorist

Building Blocks

♥ Confiding in friends is important, but when you need advice, go to parents or respected adult friends. ♥ To do well in school and in life: be positive, be alert, be prepared, be a participant! ♥ Have confidence! Be proud! Stand tall! ♥ Challenge yourself. ♥ Looking good is not as important as being good. ♥ Practice! Practice! Practice! ♥ Anger is OKAY—learn to express it correctly. ♥ Life is not always fair. ♥ Never forget—your body belongs to YOU. ♥

❤ Learn how to set goals. ❤ Reflect on the things you like about yourself, your family, your friends, your teachers, etc.—be positive. ❤ Self-reliance, self-respect and independence are the greatest gifts your parents can give you! ❤ If you borrow an item, return it promptly; refilled and in the same or better condition. ❤ Clean up after yourself—at home, at school, in public. ❤ Take your hat off indoors. ❤ Be on time. ❤

There is only one word
for being a good
communicator:
learn to LISTEN.

Christopher Morley
1890 - 1957
American novelist, journalist, essayist

Hold yourself responsible
for a higher standard than
anyone else expects of you.

Henry Ward Beecher
1813 - 1887
American cleric, editor

More Building Blocks

Be patient with yourself—it is not possible to be the best at everything. Know your strengths and accept your weaknesses. ❤ Trust your instincts—don't allow yourself to be intimidated by people or circumstances.. ❤ Tell the truth. ❤ Ask for help when you need it. ❤ Be yourself—everyone else is taken. ❤ Live up to your responsibilities to yourself, to your family and to your community. ❤

♥ Enjoy yourself. It is wonderful to be alone without feeling lonely. ♥ Question. ♥ Slow down. Take your time. ♥ Turn off the T.V. ♥ Be modest. ♥ Say "I'll try!" and "I can!", not "I can't." ♥ Be comfortable saying "No!" ♥ Remember that "No" means "No"...whether you are saying it or someone else is. ♥ Your happiness should not come at the expense of your health or safety. ♥

If we are to live together in peace, we must come to know each other better.

Lyndon B. Johnson
1908 - 1973
36th American President

When you work hard and apply yourself, you succeed. It's really not that complicated.

R. David Thomas
1932 -
Senior Chairman of Wendy's
International, Inc.

The buck stops here!

Harry S. Truman
1884 - 1972
33rd American President

Perhaps the most valuable result of all education is the ability to make your~self do the thing you have to do, when it ought to be done, whether you like it or not.

Thomas Henry Huxley
1825 - 1895
English biologist, teacher, author

73

You give but little
when you give
of your possessions.
It is when you give of
yourself that you truly give.

Kahlil Gibran
1883 - 1931
Syrian poet, novelist, essayist, painter

The secret of all learning
is patience...

Iris Murdoch
1919 -
Irish author

W hat life means to us
is determined not so much
by what life brings to us,
as by the attitude we bring
to life; not so much by what
happens to us, as by our
reaction to what happens.

Lewis L. Dunnington

...For this thing we call "failure" is not the falling down, but the staying down.

Mary Pickford
1893 - 1979
American actress

We ought to do good to
others as simply and
as naturally
as a horse runs or a bee
makes honey...

Marcus Aurelius
121 - 180
Roman Emperor and religious
philosopher

To be meek, patient,
tactful, modest, honorable,
brave is not to be either
manly or womanly;
it is to be humane.

Jane Harrison
1850 - 1928
English classical scholar

Those who bring sunshine
to the lives of others
cannot keep it
from themselves.

James M. Barrie
1860 - 1937
Scottish actor, author

83

Kid-Iquette

♥ Say PLEASE and THANK YOU —often! ♥ Greet bus drivers and others pleasantly—say, "Thank you" when you arrive at your destination. ♥ Remember people's names—use them. ♥ Use "YES," not "Yeah." ♥ Say "Excuse me," when necessary. ♥ Be a good listener—pay attention. ♥ Speak clearly —don't mumble. ♥ Use the phone politely—identify yourself right away. ♥

♥ Be assertive —stand up for yourself— but be polite. ♥ Use your humor to amuse others, not to abuse others. ♥ Compliment others. ♥ Have a firm handshake. ♥ Send Thank-You notes promptly. ♥ Compromise. ♥ Cooperate. ♥ Call if you will be later than expected. ♥ Hold doors open for others. ♥ Share. ♥ Take turns. ♥ Be patient—allow others to get off elevators, trains, buses, etc., before getting on. ♥ Offer your seat to someone more in need. ♥

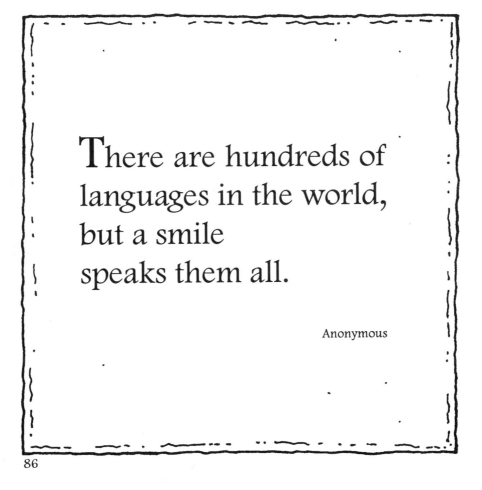

There are hundreds of
languages in the world,
but a smile
speaks them all.

Anonymous

Even if you're on the
right track,
you'll get run over
if you just sit there.

Will Rogers
1879 - 1935
American actor, humorist

To err is human;
to forgive–divine.

Alexander Pope
1688 - 1744
English poet, satirist

We must use time
creatively
and forever realize
that the time is
always ripe to do right.

Martin Luther King, Jr.
1929 - 1968
American clergyman, civil rights leader

Never look down on anybody unless you're helping them up.

Jesse Jackson
1941 -
American Baptist minister,
civil rights activist, politician

It had long since come to my attention that people of accomplishment rarely sat back and let things happen to them. They went out and happened to things.

Elinor Smith
1911 -
American aviator, author

My Space

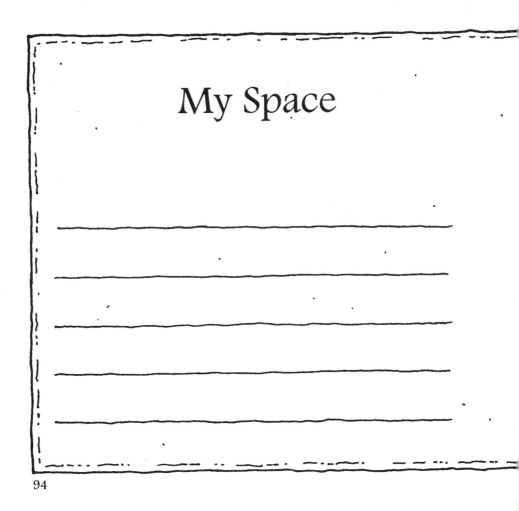